Book 1:
Debt Free Forever
BY J.J. Jones

&

Book 2:
Money Management Makeover
BY J.J. Jones

&

Book 3:
Single Women & Finances
BY J.J. Jones

Book 1:
Debt Free Forever
BY J.J. JONES

The Ultimate Guide to "Knowing Nothing to Having Everything in Financial Freedom, Becoming a Millionaire, and Becoming Debt Free Forever"

Finances Box Set #8: Debt Free Forever + Money Management Makeover + Single Women & Finances

Copyright 2014 by J.J. Jones - All rights reserved.

In no way is it legal to reproduce, duplicate, or transmit any part of this document in either electronic means or in printed format. Recording of this publication is strictly prohibited and any storage of this document is not allowed unless with written permission from the publisher. All rights reserved.

Finances Box Set #8: Debt Free Forever + Money Management Makeover + Single Women & Finances

Table of Contents

Introduction 5

Chapter 1: Why and How Deep are You in Debt? 6

Chapter 2: Income vs. Expense 7

Chapter 3: Viable Alternatives (BK, foreclosure, debt consolidation, etc.) 11

Chapter 4: Common Pitfalls (Get Rich Quick Schemes) 15

Chapter 5: Concentrate on Increasing Income 16

Chapter 6: Keep at It (zero debt) 17

Chapter 7: Financial Education and business Planning 18

Conclusion 20

Finances Box Set #8: Debt Free Forever + Money Management Makeover + Single Women & Finances

Introduction

I want to thank you and congratulate you for purchasing the book, Debt Free Forever The Ultimate Guide to "Knowing Nothing to Having Everything in Financial Freedom, Becoming a Millionaire, and Becoming Debt Free Forever".

This book contains proven steps and strategies to get you out of debt, help you stay out of debt, and then lead you to financial stability.

This three step process is essential. This is because, much like anything else you do in life, you should not stop at the halfway point. And that is what getting out of debt really is! The other part of being debt free is to become financially stable, so much so that you can live a fulfilling life, afford an adequate lifestyle, and be free from the limitations that your current financial status, shackles you in!

To be perfectly up front, there is no secret formula that is too good to be true. All there is to becoming debt free is knowing what has worked for hundreds of debt ridden consumers. Learning to tweak what works to fully fit your situation. Then, following through with your personalized debt free road map. And making sure you do not repeat the mistakes of your debt ridden past!

Thanks again for purchasing this book, I hope you enjoy it!

Chapter 1: Why and How Deep are You in Debt?

Before you can determine what type of plan will work for you, first you need to determine the reasons you got into debt in the first place. Be absolutely honest with yourself here! This is because, the efficacy of the plan you utilize, is determined by the accuracy and truth of your assessment. Tip: take your time when making the assessment. Dig deep, and add notes to your list of debts, i.e. was it a failed endeavor, a home foreclosure, a foolish spur of the moment splurge, or a necessary expense like hospitalization fee, did you lose your job, etc.

Debt Free Journal

At this point, you want to dedicate a notebook, journal, or electronic file for your entire journey. This way you know where you are starting from. You can constantly monitor where you are at. And, you fix your eye on that debt free goal.

Accumulated Debt?

How long did it take you to get to this low point? This realization can help you better assess, the reason for your financial woes. For example: you started incurring debt as soon as you lost your job. You tried to make ends meet with a part time job, and kept up appearances by charging heavily on your credit card.

How Much Exactly?

List down "ALL" your debts. It would help a lot if you could list them down from the most interest accruing, oldest debt, biggest single debt amount, etc. Make sure to have a separate sum for: due and demandable debts; about to be due (1 month or less), future collectibles, etc. Tip: if you know how to use Microsoft Excel, or any similar computer program, this should make your life a lot easier!

30% Rule

If you take 30% of your monthly income (assuming you have income), How long will it take for you to pay for all your debts? This should provide you with a rough estimate. Of course, if you have disposable, liquid assets, then the timeframe should be accelerated.

Finances Box Set #8: Debt Free Forever + Money Management Makeover + Single Women & Finances

Chapter 2: Income vs. Expenses

An income vs. expense worksheet is necessary for you to determine how much of your income are you spending. You can utilize your I&E worksheet in several ways. This includes but is not limited to:

- Knowing how much you actually spend vis a vis how much of that spending you can cut off.
- Knowing how much income you still need
- Pinpointing the area where you spend the most and then determining whether or not it coincides with your priorities.

Common sense says that you can spend as much as you make in a month. But common sense is not very practical. That is, if you want to get out of debt and eventually earn millions.

30% Surplus

In reality, it is a good idea to save up at least 20% to 30% of your monthly net income. Leave that untouched and deposit it in your savings account for a rainy day! Anything below 20% and you are overspending way beyond your means, or you are not earning enough income.

Sources of Income

"ALL" sources of income must be considered. From your salary, income on rental property, interest income, etc.

What Income to Include?

If you are the sole provider for the household, then you include your total net income. This is gross income minus taxes. If you have another member of the household who fully shares his/her income to the household i.e. spouse, then add their net income as well.

If another member of the family shares only part of their income, then only add that to the total net income. Make sure to only include regular contributions. For example:

Mr. A 2,000 net monthly

Mrs. A 1,500 net monthly

Son A 300 monthly contribution

Total Expenses

For accurate results it would be best if you had receipts for your expenses. Tip: if you enroll certain accounts online, then you have easy access to your tabulated expenses i.e. Credit cards.

Miscellaneous Expenses

Make sure to include all expenditures. For example: miscellaneous expenses that you might have overlooked. This includes paper money you had to exchange or buy gum or buy bottled water with, for spare coins you need. You then whittle away at your expenses until you only have spare change for unnecessaries and 99% of your spending is fully identifiable.

Tip: any money you can't account for, when balancing your income and expenses goes to miscellaneous. This way you actually see how much of a sinkhole your unnecessary expenses are.

Savings Account

You need to deposit that 30%, preferably more of your income on a bank account. This gets credited to your list of expenses. This way you are creating a good credit standing with your bank, to offset, at least to a certain extent, other declared debts you might have. Perform a general cleaning in your home and collect all your spare and unnecessary change. Deposit these as well!

Tightening the Belt

Look at your income and expense worksheet. Try to remove anything or minimize any and every area in your spending. For example:

Minimize takeout and start cooking meals. Minimize meat purchases and balance it out with fruits and veggies. Stop buying fizzy and sugary drinks. All you really need is water. In this regard, tap water is usually safe for drinking! Bottled water really is unnecessary! Also:

- Gas expense can be minimized by commuting once in a while. Walking or using your bike when doing small errands also helps.
- Do you really need that new cellular postpaid plan? Why not keep your old phone, minimize calls by texting, and consolidating your internet plan.
- Do you really need cable TV? Most of the things you watch anyway you can get online!

Things You Can't Skimp On

Regular home maintenance, auto insurance, tuition fees, taxes, regular medical checkups, etc. are things you cannot skimp on! Pay these on time and in full!

For example: Real estate insurance or other one time payments per annum must be factored into your expenses, divided into as many months, as the next installment. So if you still have 6 months to go, you can divide it in 6 monthly expense cycles. Never utilize your savings account for this. Your savings account is only to be used to pay debts and for emergencies.

Talk to Your Debtor

The last thing you want is to forget about the debt. The best thing to do is to talk to your creditor and ask for an extension. Even if this is not possible, keeping lines open can save you lots of troubles in the near future.

Freeze Interest Rates

If your creditor is a private person, maybe you can ask for an extension, without payment of interest. Explain your situation fully.

If your debtor is a bank or lending institution, there may be a grace period clause you can use. Although, be absolutely sure about using the grace period since this is most likely a onetime deal.

Switching debts

You can also ask if some demandable debts can be converted into a loan, i.e. A credit card debt converted to a personal bank loan. The interest rate is usually lower and you get to pay installments.

Mortgages

If you have a mortgage then you need to start thinking of how important that mortgage is to you and your capacity to pay. Your rule of thumb is to keep only what you can pay for and prioritize your needs.

For example

A family home is important, but if you cannot really afford the home then, maybe it's better to let go while you're able to. Do you really need that automobile? Remember you need to factor in amortizations, gas, upkeep, insurance, etc. If you can go to and from work via commute, then, maybe letting go of that car is the right thing to do.

If you have spare properties, then it is best to let go of the same to pay for debts. I.e. A second home, second automobile, expensive jewelry, etc.

But you need to learn when to let go and when to hang on to your properties. A good rule of thumb is to factor in interest payments and penalties. Then determine if lowering the asking price will allow you to save money or not.

Finances Box Set #8: Debt Free Forever + Money Management Makeover + Single Women & Finances

To be perfectly honest, if you can pay your debts by selling peripheral or spare properties, then do it! But if selling your property only cuts less than 50% of your debts, then you need to look for other alternatives first.

Chapter 3: Viable Alternatives

Let us assume that you looked into your income and expense worksheet, you looked into your savings account, and you even factored in your real and personal properties. You've also contacted your relatives. But you are still short of paying "ALL" your debts. You need a little bit of help from a third party. Below are a few financial tools that you can utilize.

Real/Personal Property Mortgage

If you don't want to sell your property outright, you can mortgage it. Some authors will even tell you that taking out a second or third mortgage are alternatives. This author is of the opinion that you should NOT take out a second or third mortgage.

As a general rule, you stick to 1 mortgage per property. This is because; in most cases it will result in you making your debts more complicated! Best case scenario, you delay the demand ability of the debt. Worst case scenario, you lose another property, you get buried in more debt, more interest payments, and more penalties.

When mortgaging a property, always sign a deal on the winning side. This means you know you can handle the amortizations. You know you can keep the property. You know you can pay your debts in full.

Refinance

A refinance is a secondary mortgage that takes the place of the old mortgage. This can be from the same lender or different lender. A refinance is a viable alternative for those who are in a better position to renegotiate their loan terms. This includes, but is not limited to:

- A better credit report and score
- A better economy
- Promotional refinance rates
- A substantial down payment you've saved up
- You qualify for government mandated/regulated repayment plans

Fixed Rate All the Way

A caveat, you always want to know how much you will pay on the loan from the first amortization to the last amortization! So, whenever you apply for any loan or refinance your loan, it is almost always a good idea to make sure that your interest payments are fixed. Yes, there are a couple of exemptions wherein you can opt for adjustable rate mortgages and/or balloon payments, but these are very rare cases.

Debt Consolidation

Debt consolidation is a viable alternative for debtors who get confused by the many debts they have. Think about it, isn't it easier to pay just 1 loan with one interest rate and due once every month; as opposed to several loans, due on different dates, with different interest rates, from different lenders.

Aside from being convenient, lumping all your loans into one, may also afford you the advantage of a lower total interest rate. This means, the sum total of all your interest earning debts minus all your debtors, is higher, than the interest rate offered by a single lender.

It is always a good idea to consolidate "ALL" debts into one. But in some cases, you can leave out a couple of debts from the loan. It really is up to you and the advantages you can get form the consolidation.

No Longer Due

When you consolidate a loan, due debts become future debts. The total loan amount is divided into as many installments you and your lender agreed to. So you get a little bit of breathing room for at least a month.

More Onerous

Take note however, that one big debt is more destructive to your credit score, especially if it is a consolidation loan. This is not really a threat if you will be paying on time and in full. But if you default, then literally trouble begins to occur. Pay special attention to an acceleration clause. And at the very least, default in one consolidation loan and other lenders will be hesitant to provide you another one.

Simply put, this alternative is viable for a consumer who is in debt partly because of negligence, lack of skill in budgeting, and who might have experienced a temporary hardship in his/her finances.

Bankruptcy

There are several types of bankruptcy filing. This article will discuss the 2 most common types of private individuals, as debtors. Bear in mind that bankruptcy is not a magic pill. Not everyone is allowed to take it and not everyone will get "better" because of it. But if taken by the right consumer with proper planning and due execution, it can save you from overwhelming debt.

Means Test

This test initially determines what type of bankruptcy you can file for, or if you can file for one to begin with. The BK court will then assess the filer to determine if the BK will be allowed to prosper or should be dismissed.

Credit Rating and BK

There are a lot of "so called" experts who tell you that BK will ruin your credit report. News, flash, the fact that you are already buried in debt also ruins your BK. Yes your filing will make your credit score drop some more, but chances are, it will drop to that same low, even lower, if you keep bleeding due and demandable debts. Think of BK as an amputation of a limb. If you don't amputate, you'll die due to blood lost and or infection. The only plus side to a BK, is whatever you lose, you can eventually get back!

Yes, BK will last for 7 to 10 years depending on the type of BK and the length of the repayment plan. Within that same timeframe your facility of credit will be limited.

Lawyer of Self filing?

In theory, a person can file for BK without the help of a professional and/or lawyer. The forms and instructions are available for free via Bankruptcy courts, or online. In reality, only those with limited assets, "ALL" within the same state can realistically file for BK "pro se" (by themselves) i.e. a house, a car, some cash, etc. If you have several properties, some of which are out of state, then you need to at least hire professional and state licensed BK filers or lawyers.

Automatic Stay?

An automatic stay means creditors who do not hold a security over your property, cannot go after you, while your Bankruptcy filing is being heard by the BK court. Do not believe everything you hear. Yes, a BK filing can allow you to stop a bank from executing/foreclosing on your property, but only for the time being. This is because a bank or creditor has a mortgage or security clause that the BK court must respect. The best it can do is stay foreclosed for a couple of months. All the creditor does is file a petition in court showing a better right, then they can continue with the foreclosure.

Chapter 7

Also known as liquidation BK. As a general rule, any property not declared as exempt and not requested to be excluded is included in the BK filing. Chapter 7 is most applicable for those who have overwhelming debt, and have no capacity to pay.

Exceptions both as to type and amount depend on the state where you live. At the very least, a modest family home, unattached by any independent creditor can be exempted. So are modest clothing, furniture, professional articles, limited cash, etc.

Chapter 13

This is also known as repayment BK. The filer/debtor has financial capacity, but inability to pay the full amount of all debts. The creditors do not want to negotiate so the court steps in. Usually this involves cutting off the interest payments and penalties from all debts. Repayment usually lasts a couple to several years. While you are under repayment you need to pay on time and in full, lest your creditors find a hole they can exploit!

Chapter 4: Common Pitfalls (Get Rich Quick Schemes)

When trying to get out of debt, you need the right type of information, the right type of remedy, the proper plan of attack and a steady hand to follow thru until the last payment. The problem is, there are so many ways you can get things wrong. Below are a few things to steer clear of.

Who to Listen to

You don't want to listen to any Tom, Dick, or Harry. You want someone who has been there and done that! The author of this eBook is one such person. He started off as a debtor, crippled by credit card debts, a car loan, and a home mortgage. He was literally crawling form one paycheck to another. It took a while but eventually, all debts were paid.

Too Good to be True

It probably is! There is no easy way to get out of debt, especially substantial debt. You really need to tighten your belt and rack your brains. There is: no secret formula, no secret technique your creditors don't want you to know, no single tip that is so effective it should be illegal. Stay the course of paying your debts!

The Road You Take

Getting a refinance when in fact you know you are stretching things is a bad idea. Filing for BK when you can actually pay, will lead to a dismissal of your case. Tightening your budget when it is already so tight you are living a miserable life is also a bad idea. There are several financial tools you can utilize to get out of debt. Find that proper tool and utilize it!

Tip: consult with a credit counselor. The same counselor you will need a certificate from to file for BK. These individuals are state licensed and are neutral third parties. They can advice you on your viable alternatives based on your personal and financial situation.

Payday Loans

Simply put, payday lending is a bad idea. The interest rate is off the charts, and the ability to get instant cash is addictive to some individuals. And you have better alternatives. Chances are you still have a credit card, why not use that instead. But only in cases of emergencies!

Service Providers

You either buy a book to know what to do or hire the services of someone who will do everything for you. You don't buy a book with a service at a bloated cost, so someone can talk to you over the phone and "guide" you thru your problems. Heck, better call a credit counselor!

Chapter 5: Concentrate on Increasing Income

As mentioned earlier, you can only tighten the belt so much! You need to realize that you are budgeting to streamline your spending and to instill a discipline in yourself. When money is still short, and most probably it will be, then an additional source of income is the better alternative. Below are a few ideas.

Ask for a Salary Increase

If you come on time, rarely get absent, have excellent performance, then a raise is in order. Most companies have an assessment every 6 months to 2 years. When is your next assessment? Prepare for it! And make sure your company does provide for a salary increase.

Get a New Job

You'd be surprised that most debtors are employed. The problem is, they are under employed or are working on a dead end job. Here is a good rule of thumb. If you have been working for the same company for 3 years with no salary increase, with very little to do, and nothing important to contribute, then better get out! You want a job where you matter! Where you are part of the decision making! Where a salary increase for good performance is a sure thing!

Part Time Job

While you are looking for your dream job, you might as well augment your income by getting a part time job. The trend nowadays is to get an online job. This way you can go home, be with your kids, and still sneak in a couple of hours of work. If you are the man/woman of the house, then an online job allows you to add to your household's income, while still being able to take care of the kids or your elderly parents. Pick an online job that fits your skill and interest. You have dozens of options: transcription, teaching, back office documentation, auditing, content writing, website design and/or maintenance, marketing.

A Caveat

You are looking for an online job to make money, not part with your money! So steer clear of multi level marketing schemes, membership schemes, forex, bitcoin, stocks, etc. Simply put, anything that requires you to pay money first to get money is a no-no. No matter how tempting the offer is!

Chapter 6: Keep at It

Admit it, you are reading this eBook, thinking to yourself "This is easy, I can do that!" Yes you can! But several months into your well thought out plan, you start to cheat, with one credit card charge here, a new flagship android or Mac phone there, a designer pair of jeans here, and you're back to racking up debts!

Go back to your journal! Remember how bad things got! Don't let that happen again. You need to get to zero debt before making a substantial purchase! Heck, a smart phone can last you 3 to 5 years before it conks out. You're old jalopy can last even longer. Clothes, you can occasionally buy some, but only non signature brands and timed during big sale dates. You can splurge from time to time with food. This way you don't feel deprived, but only within reason and within budget!

Go Easy on the Credit Card

You do not need to cut your credit cards. At least, not unless you have more than three. Keep the most useful and oldest cards. Not necessarily the ones with the highest credit limit. Only use it for groceries, gas, and important purchases. Make use of the convenient points that you get.

Celebrate Milestones

Every month you successfully stick to your plan, order a box of pizza, or celebrate with a reasonably priced bottle of wine. Anything to tide you over for the long haul! This should keep your spirit up until you become debt free.

Chapter 7: Financial Education and Business Planning

Knowing how to handle your finances is a tricky endeavor. Sure you can do it by yourself, but it will be a trial and error thing. You have no time for that. While paying off your debts, look for worthwhile seminars. Nope, none of that universe crap! Get something more practical like accounting 101, consumer tax laws and how to use them to your advantage, or tax shielding, etc.

The Ultimate Goal

Remember, you want to be a millionaire, after you pay off your debts. How do you expect to handle that kind of money without proper schooling! At the very least, your financial education can provide you necessary certifications and contacts if and when you set up your own business!

Why Put Up a Business?

Your goal is to be a millionaire! The fastest way to that goal is thru your own business! So, what are you good at, what is your passion, what are you educated for? Remember that savings account? Aside from using that for your debt payments, you can also use that to put up a modest business.

Social Media Helps

Nowadays, a physical store location is no longer necessary. Put up shop at home. Make sure you have the appropriate certificates. Potential customers can visit you in a homey looking nook. Get some professional looking pictures. Don't pay someone; chances are you have a relative who has a professional grade camera! Now advertise online. Tap your family, relatives, friends, etc. Now use their social network to increase your coverage. Remember, your goal is to set up shop with minimal capital outlay. Most of your funds should be used for your goods, or inventory!

Tip: put up a dedicated page for your business. Link social media outlets like Facebook, twitter, Instagram, SalesForce, LinkedIn etc.

Simple Value

All you need is a product that meets a certain human need. It has to be cheaper, do things better, or in a different way than your competition. Now run with it! Try a viral ad campaign on YouTube, Instagram, tweeter, etc. now set up several ads, and see what works and what does not.

Price Wars?

If you don't have a unique product, or if there are other sellers who have a different version of your product, the last thing you want is to cut prices to try and undermine the competition. This can lead to a price war that is bad for business. What you should do is try to carve your own following. Remember, with the social media generation it's all about lifestyle and branding.

Go Local First

Identify your product or service with your locality. Again use social media to carve out a local following. This should set you apart from out of town and state sellers/services. Personally interact with buyers. This increases your support and the information you get can be useful in version 2 of your product and/or service.

Go to Conventions

Visit conventions showcasing your business. Get ideas from them! See if you can widen your product or service base with some of the ideas and contacts you get from that convention. Your next step is to put up shop in a convention hall.

Conclusion

Thank you again for purchasing this book!

I hope this book was able to help you to: realize that there is a way out of overwhelming debt; you need to outfit yourself with the right tools, and execute the right plan; you need to follow thru until you have zero debt; and, you need to step things up a notch and augment your income!

The next step is to go back to your journal. Re-read the eBook to get more insight, add some more notes. Now consult with a debt counselor! Pay the minimal fee, and make sure to get the certificate you need, just in case you need to file for BK in the near future.

Remember, getting out of debt is not a race. It is a marathon that requires mental toughness and endurance. You should pace yourself, don't run out of steam midway thru!

Finally, if you enjoyed this book, please take the time to share your thoughts and post a review on Amazon. We do our best to reach out to readers and provide the best value we can. Your positive review will help us achieve that. It'd be greatly appreciated!

Thank you and good luck!

Book 2:
Money Management Makeover
BY J.J. JONES

The Ultimate Plan for Financial Success with Managing Your Money by Budgeting and Saving!

Finances Box Set #8: Debt Free Forever + Money Management Makeover + Single Women & Finances

Copyright 2014 by J.J. Jones - All rights reserved.

In no way is it legal to reproduce, duplicate, or transmit any part of this document in either electronic means or in printed format. Recording of this publication is strictly prohibited and any storage of this document is not allowed unless with written permission from the publisher. All rights reserved.

Finances Box Set #8: Debt Free Forever + Money Management Makeover + Single Women & Finances

Table Of Contents

Introduction 24

Chapter 1 - Assess Your Current Financial Situation......................... 25

Chapter 2 - Create a Financial Plan...27

Chapter 3 - Create a Budget Plan and Stick to It 29

Chapter 4 - Get Rid of Debt ASAP 33

Chapter 5 - Safeguard Yourself and Your Money 35

Chapter 6 - Put Your Money in Investments.......................................37

Conclusion 39

Introduction

I want to thank you and congratulate you for purchasing the book, *"Money Management Makeover - The Ultimate Plan for Financial Success with Managing Your Money by Budgeting and Saving"*.

This book contains proven steps and strategies on how to assess your current financial situation and make sound plans in order to get rid of debt, start an emergency fund, and achieve your financial goals. This book will help you get started on budgeting, saving and investing your money to gain financial wealth and freedom.

Thanks again for purchasing this book, I hope you enjoy it!

Finances Box Set #8: Debt Free Forever + Money Management Makeover + Single Women & Finances

Chapter 1 - Assess Your Current Financial Situation

If you want to become financially stable but don't know where to begin, then you should start by first determining your exact financial health status. You need to be able to identify how much money you have, how much you owe, and how much you need to have. Knowing these facts will help you create changes to improve your finances and achieve your goals.

Step 1: Create Financial Statements

There are two types of financial statements that you will need, and these are cash flow statement and net worth statement.

Cash-Flow Statement. This information is a comparison between your monthly net income and your average monthly expenses. You begin creating your cash flow statement by listing down all of your monthly expenses and then adding up the total amount of monthly expenses. After that, you list down all of your monthly net income (deductions not included) and add them all up as well. Deduct the total amount of monthly expenses from the total amount of your income. The difference defines your current cash flow.

Your current cash flow can help you determine what changes need to be made in order to increase the amount. This will entail you to create a budget, increase your income, and minimize your expenses if your goal is to save more money.

The following are common income sources: salary, earnings from part-time jobs, child support and alimony

Common monthly expenses are: rent or mortgage, food and groceries, utilities, medical expenses, property taxes, home maintenance costs, insurance, savings and investment contributions, credit cards, child care and child support, clothing, loans, memberships, transportation, and leisure.

Net Worth Statement. Your net worth is your total assets in comparison to your total liabilities. Assets are your cash, property and other valuable items. Your liabilities are the money that you owe.

Assets are in the form of: cash (including the amount in your checking and savings accounts), collectibles, Certificates of Deposits or CODs, Money Market Funds, Life insurance cash value, real estate market value, business property or assets, personal valuables (such as gold and silver), and retirement accounts.

Liabilities are: bills, credit card balances, loan balances, mortgage balances, taxes owed and home-equity credit lines.

Step 2: Organize and Review Your Financial Records

Create a filing system (both soft and hard copies) of your financial records to keep in track. Form a habit of regularly updating it. You should also include your partner or spouse's financial records.

The files to be included are all of your bank, loan, credit card and investment accounts, your legal documents including insurance policies, real estate titles and tax files, your billing statements and correspondents, and other important documents such as your Social Security retirement and other benefits.

After you have successfully organized all of your financial records, you can start reviewing them to help you pinpoint where you are losing money and where you can save money. This includes knowing your current credit status and how to fix any problems that you might have. Also, determine how much you currently can afford in case of a financial crisis.

Now that you have a clear view of your current financial situation, you can move on to creating a financial plan as well as a solid budget.

Chapter 2 - Create a Financial Plan

A solid financial plan should be organized and written down. It is your guide to achieving your financial goals each step of the way. It also serves as a reminder of your financial responsibilities towards yourself and your future.

Steps in Creating a Financial Plan

Step 1: Set your financial goals

Think about what you really want to achieve in short-term and long-term. These might include further education for yourself or college education for your children, plans in getting a promotion or setting up your own business, buying a new house or moving to a new place, and the lifestyle that you wish to maintain after you retire. You can also include leisure goals such as going on a vacation.

Step 2: Make an estimate of your projected income

Most likely one of your financial goals is to increase your income. You can distinguish the different sources of income based on five major categories: career, business, investments, inheritance and unexpected income. Keep in mind that it is always best to have more than one income source.

Career income is when you are the one who is employed and received fixed salary.

Business income is when you profit from running your own business or from products or services that you generate.

Investments are your stocks, bonds, money market funds, real estate and CODs.

Inheritance is money coming from other people.

Unexpected income is money coming from bonuses, gifts, lottery winnings and other similar sources. You should already have a financial plan ready for when you do receive unexpected income so that you will not end up spending it away, and instead help make it grow even bigger.

Step 3: Create a timeline for your goals

With each financial goal that you have, come up with concrete steps on how to achieve them. You should also create "deadlines" for each of these steps so that you will be reminded of what to do each day in order to bring you closer to your goals.

Your goals should be divided into four main categories: immediate future (within 12 months), near future (5 year span), extended future (10 year span), and distant future (after ten years).

Step 4: Develop an income strategy that will help you achieve your goals based on your timeline. You will also need a solid budget and an expenses and allotment tracker to prevent yourself from overspending on unnecessary expenses.

Step 5: Come up with a way to fully commit yourself to your financial plan. A lot of people create very good financial plans but do not follow them, mainly because they become swayed into spending on things that they do not need and throwing themselves off track.

Chapter 3 - Create a Budget Plan and Stick to It

A budget is technically the amount of money that you allocate for specific purposes, particularly your basic needs. Most people make the mistake of treating their budget as a "suggestion" instead of a rule, which is why their liabilities constantly increase and their net worth decreases.

The tool to increasing your wealth is your income, and the best way to handle your income power is with a monthly budget. Not having a budget is like letting water flow carelessly in all directions, and before you know it you will have ended up with nothing. The budgets are the channels that control the flow of water. You decide how big the channels are, where they are heading.

The Habit of Creating a Monthly Budget

You have made a wise decision to plan how you will be spending your money. Creating a budget is a habit. In fact, you will need to create a new budget for the next month at the end of the current month. After all, each month presents different agendas, from holidays, birthdays, insurance bills, and whatnot. It is difficult - if not impossible - to stick to a single budget plan all of the time. Plan to create a new monthly budget a day or two before the start of each month so that you can treat each month as a fresh start.

Practice the Zero-based Budget Strategy

Zero-based budget is to make sure that the difference between your income and the outgo is zero. If you have paid for all the expenses and you have some money left (say, 300 dollars) you are not finished with your budget yet. You must be able to tell where it will go - such as paying off your debts, putting it in your emergency fund or investing it - or else you will spend it on a liability purchase.

Statistics show that those who follow a zero-based budget were able to pay off 19 percent more of their debt and save 18 percent more of their money compared to those who do not follow it.

Avoid Wasteful Money Burners

If your expenses far outweigh your income, then you will need to get rid of some spending habits. Even if you do increase your income substantially you will still end up spending a lot more if you stick to old, overspending habits.

For instance, impulse shopping is one major money burning habit. If it's not in your list of needs, do not purchase it no matter how "great" the deal is. You will figure out a way to buy it in the future when you do need it.

You shell out hundreds of dollars more each month from eating out. This monetary value is higher compared to the time you have "saved" from preparing your own meals. Learn how to plan your meals ahead and shop for cheap but healthy ingredients.

Determine How Much You Need to Spend Each Month

Review your list of expenses and highlight the ones that you cannot avoid spending on, such as your rent or mortgage, insurance, transportation to and from work, utility bills, and groceries and so on. Total the amount and deduct it from your total monthly income. It would be even better if you figured out ways to lower this number as well.

For instance, you can anticipate sales, collect coupons and buy generic brands in order to minimize grocery expenses and put what you have saved into paying off your debts and eventually into your emergency fund and investments.

Think of clever ways for you and your family to stay entertained without using up too much electricity or spending on trips and such.

Learn to swap items with friends and neighbours instead of always buying to avoid additional purchases, such as clothes and tools.

After you have determined the expenses for your needs, divide the remaining amount between saving up for your emergency fund, paying off debt and your wants. The rule of thumb is to set aside 60 percent for expenses for your needs, 20 percent to pay off debt (and eventually to put into your emergency fund and investments), and 20 percent for your wants.

The 5 Basic Steps of a Budget Plan

There are 5 basic steps in a budget plan. Each step will require you to make several changes in your current lifestyle. It depends on how much change you can tolerate, but the sooner you increase your allotment for savings and investments the sooner you will gain financial wealth.

Step 1: Create a starter emergency fund

It is very important to have some money set aside for emergencies. The recommended amount is 1,000 dollars to cover minor emergencies. However, you need to start building this immediately so that you can pay off your debts as soon as possible.

A good suggestion in increasing the amount of money allotted to your starter emergency fund is to try to save around 10 percent of your budget and put it into your starter. This is in addition to the 20 percent that you set aside for it. For example, if your budget for your groceries is 500 dollars, figure out a way to lower it to 450 dollars so that you can put the 50 dollars into your starter.

Step 2: Pay off all of your debts

In chapter 4 you will learn how to get rid of debt. It is very important to get rid of your debts as soon as possible otherwise the interest will just compound and you will end up paying for much, much more than the value of the items that you paid for on credit.

For example, if you bought a towel with your credit card for 20 dollars, the cost of your 20 dollar quality budget will turn into 60 dollars within a few months' time if you do not pay off your credit card debts right now.

Step 3: Fully fund your emergency fund

After you have paid off all of your debts, you can now move on to building an emergency fund. This will be discussed in detail in Chapter 5.

Step 4: Start investing for retirement

It is inevitable that we will all age and not be as able-bodied as we used to, that is why we need to save up for this part of our lives. After you have fully funded your emergency fund, you will need to start setting aside some money for a long-term investment in order to reap the rewards 10 to 40 years from now.

Step 5: Start investing for your personal financial goals

Your budget should accommodate the money that you would like to set aside for your personal financial goals. Review your financial plan and your timeframe so that you can plan your budget around these goals.

Budgeting Habits to Make

Budgeting is not about depriving yourself. It is about being careful with where your money is going, so that you do not end up getting robbed of a financially stable future. Develop these sound spending and budgeting habits to help make things go smoothly for you:

Monitor and analyze your spending regularly.

It is important to start the habit of taking note of your expenses in a personal ledger and to compare it with how much your overall income is. It might sound tedious but it actually won't take more than 5 minutes of your time. By tracking what you spend every day, you will be able to identify unnecessary expenditures and avoid them in the future. Remember, a small hole can sink a big ship.

Determine how much more you will be able to save every month.

Instead of thinking about how to spend your money, it is best to start thinking about how you are going to be able to save more money. Even better if you start thinking how to earn even more money. Be creative and frugal in spending for your needs and wants. For example, learn to negotiate in order to get discounts and freebies, and look for cheaper places where you can regularly buy your groceries and such. Even small savings will add up if you look at the big picture.

Do not put all of your cash in the same wallet.

Even some of the most financially sound individuals find it very difficult not to be tempted to spend their money on something. If you know that you tend to make impulse buys, you will be able to avoid it by not bringing all of your cash with you wherever you go. Also, if you are going someplace without meaning to buy anything (such as going out for coffee with friends), bring only enough cash that you have set as your budget and leave your credit cards behind.

Save first before spending.

Most people still have the old habit of spending first before and then save up what is left, if any. Whenever acquire income, make it a habit to head straight to the bank and make a deposit into your savings first before you buy anything. This will help keep things in perspective, because sometimes people become overwhelmed with their income and start to think of how they will spend this much money when in fact the remaining amount for their wants is minimal compared to how much they should save to achieve their financial goals.

Chapter 4 - Get Rid of Debt ASAP

The key to getting out of debt is to start paying off the smallest first in order to start a momentum. This might sound contrary to the common notion that you should start paying off the debt with the highest interest but it is actually highly effective. It is called the Snowball Method and it has much to do with human behaviour.

When you start paying off your smaller debts first, you become motivated to move on to the bigger ones after you have crossed them off of your list. After you have accumulated 1,000 dollars in a passbook or checking account for your starter emergency fund, concentrate and make an effort to pay off all of your debt as soon as possible (except the mortgage).

Step 1: List Down Your Debts

The first step is to make a list of all of your debts, starting with the smallest balance. Do not think about the interest rates or terms, but if there are two debts with the same payoffs, you can put the one with the higher interest rate before the other one on the list.

Step 2: Focus on the Deadline

Using your cash flow statements and budget, create a timeline on how you can pay off your debt quickly. Keep tracking how much you have paid off to build momentum on your goal to financial freedom.

Step 3: Focus on the Smallest Debt First

Concentrate all of your effort and resources to pay off the smallest debt while continuing to pay for the minimum payments of the others. Once you have completely paid off the smallest, move on to the next one down the list and do the same.

Alternative Methods to Pay Off Debt

The Snowball method is applicable for most people, but if you know for sure that you are financially disciplined you can choose to pay off your credit card debts and loans with the higher interest first in order to further minimize costs and get rid of debt even faster.

Those who cannot afford to pay all of the minimum requirements while paying off the smallest debt at the same time can also choose to pay off the debts with the higher interest rates to keep them from compounding.

Handling Consumer Debt

Do not get into deeper debt while you are paying off your debt otherwise you will be trapped in a vicious cycle. This means you should cancel all of your credit cards and keep a Visa or MasterCard debit card instead. However, if you are to apply the strategy below, you must not cancel the high-interest rate credit cards first or else your credit score will go down. Just make sure to stop using the card with the higher interest rate.

One strategy that you can apply to help lower your credit card debt interest rate is to apply for a lower-rate credit card. You will need to have a really good credit report and score to obtain this, and your debt outstanding should not have too big of a difference compared to your income. Once approved, you can transfer the outstanding balance from your higher interest rate credit cards to the lower one and start paying them off obsessively.

Another option is to negotiate for a better deal from the current credit card company. Call the bank and tell them that you want to cancel your card because you want to choose a competitor that does not have an annual fee and has a lower interest rate. Chances are the bank will match the terms of this competitor; otherwise you can go ahead and apply for the lower interest rate card before cancelling.

If you are facing extreme debt, you will need to take action immediately. This can be overwhelming so choose to seek help from a credit counselling agency. Do plenty of research on the company before getting them as some of them are funded by the feeds paid by creditors.

Ask them if they offer debt management programs, and if they do you should avoid them. A debt management program is when you are on a repayment plan with your creditors but the agency is paid a monthly fee for handling the payments. Get a specific price quote and get a contract in writing. Avoid agencies with a high upfront fee. If the agency advises that you stop paying your bills, avoid them as well as they might just take your money and disappear. Lastly ask for their license and the qualifications of their counsellors, and assurance of confidentiality and security.

Chapter 5 - Safeguard Yourself and Your Money

Once you have paid off all of your debts, you can breathe a big sigh of relief and give yourself a pat on the back for a job well done. Now you have a clean slate and move on to building your financial wealth.

Readiness and protection are very important when it comes to financial stability, this is why you will need to create an emergency fund and review your insurance plans.

Fill up your Emergency Fund

You can now concentrate on fully funding your emergency fund. Your emergency fund will help you survive through sudden financial problems such as unemployment or hospitalization. It should be enough to cover for your expenses for 3 to 6 months. Place your emergency fund in a passbook account to prevent you from touching it or spending it on less important things.

Focus on building your emergency fund up to 3 months first, and after that you can split 50 percent on funding the last 3 months and the other 50 percent on investments.

Get Insured

Minor emergencies can be covered by an emergency fund, but major ones such as calamities, illness and legal disputes can really drain your finances. The best way to protect you and your money would be to get the right insurance policy.

The ones you need the most are health insurance, disability insurance and life insurance if you have dependents.

Health Insurance Tips.

Find a good health insurance policy that has a high deductible. This is the amount of medical claims that you need to pay out first using your emergency funds before the insurance coverage pays you for it. You should also look for one with the highest co-payment. This is the amount that you need to shell out when service is rendered. A quality health insurance should have major medical coverage including laboratory work, ancillary charges and hospital care.

Disability Insurance Tips.

A disability insurance will protect your income for you, especially when you become disabled and cannot work anymore. If you are employed and have long-term disability coverage, ask the benefits department of the company that you are working for on the details of the policy and check whether it will pay benefits when you reach a certain age.

Life Insurance Tips.

If you have dependents, you will want to protect them from becoming financially burdened in case something happens to you. But if you are single, independent and do not have any children then you do not need one. It is recommended that you purchase a low cost term insurance instead of cash value insurance, because you will want to invest separately.

Chapter 6 - Put Your Money in Investments

Saving your money in a bank account alone will not help you in the long run because of inflation. The interest rates of a typical savings account are a lot less compared to inflation. Investing your hard earned money is therefore the wisest choice to make especially if you want to beat inflation. Investing takes a lot of research and discipline, but the efforts are really worth it.

There are two major ways to invest your money, the first is to lend it and gain income from interest rates and the second is to buy assets.

Lending Investments

Lending investments are in the form of bonds, treasury bills, and certificates of deposit or COD. You become a lender when you lend your money to a bank the federal government or any other organization that offers this setup. The goal is for you to get paid the interest in addition to the original investment that you have lent. There is no assurance as to whether you will indeed reap what you sow, that is why you must do plenty of research first.

Ownership Investments

The three best choices to boost your financial wealth are to invest in ownership investments, which are stocks, real estate, and small business.

Stocks are the shares of ownership that are in a company, and the most common ownership investment vehicle. You become an owner once you put your money in as an asset on real estate or a company that will generate profits. As a stockholder you get a share in the profits called dividends, which are paid quarterly to shareholders. If the company's business goes well, you gain too. Vice versa, if the business does not succeed. Do not invest in individual stocks if you do not know everything about it. Keep in mind that researching on it can become a full time job and will take up a lot of your time and some money.

If you are new to investing and would like to invest in a low-cost investment plan, research on mutual funds and exchange-traded funds or ETFs instead. Mutual funds are a collection of funds from many investors like you and the capital is invested to produce gain. ETFs are a lot like mutual funds, except they trade on a major stock exchange.

Becoming a real estate owner or investor is a financially rewarding type of ownership investment. Land is a commodity that generally steadily increases in value over time, making it a safe investment as long as you have done your research. For example, buying your own home is a good way to begin investing in real estate. The equity that will build over time will really improve your net worth.

The last ownership investment is to go into small business. You can either start your own small business or you can invest in others' small businesses and gain profit along with them. Many people have successfully achieved financial wealth while running a business. Naturally, it requires complete dedication, focus and really good ideas for it to work.

The best advice when it comes to investment is to spread the risk through diversification. It adheres to the old saying, "don't put all of your eggs in the same basket." In order to lower your risk of losing everything, allot your investment capital in different types of investments such as real estate, bonds, stocks and small businesses. You should also diversify them in both domestic and international markets. This is called asset allocation. In the long run, your decisions in asset allocation will determine the total return for your diversified portfolio.

Know how your level of risk tolerance and consider other factors in mind, such as your financial goals as well as your age. The younger you are, the more risks you will be able to cope with.

Conclusion

Thank you again for purchasing this book!

I hope this book was able to help you to plan your financial goals carefully and fully understand your current financial health.

The next step is to take action and work on achieving your financial goals. Work hard and make your money work for you as well. With discipline, determination and focus you will definitely gain the financial freedom that you deserve.

Finally, if you enjoyed this book, please take the time to share your thoughts and post a review on Amazon. We do our best to reach out to readers and provide the best value we can. Your positive review will help us achieve that. It'd be greatly appreciated!

Thank you and good luck!

Book 3:
Single Women & Finances
BY J.J.JONES

A Woman's Secret Diary To Saving, Budgeting, and Retirement

Finances Box Set #8: Debt Free Forever + Money Management Makeover + Single Women & Finances

Copyright 2014 by J.J. Jones - All rights reserved.

In no way is it legal to reproduce, duplicate, or transmit any part of this document in either electronic means or in printed format. Recording of this publication is strictly prohibited and any storage of this document is not allowed unless with written permission from the publisher. All rights reserved.

Finances Box Set #8: Debt Free Forever + Money Management Makeover + Single Women & Finances

Table of Contents

Introduction 43

Chapter 1: Advantages and Disadvantages of Being a Single Woman 44

Chapter 2: Saving Tips for a Single Woman 46

Chapter 3: Budget Tips for the Single Woman 48

Chapter 4: Retirement Tips for the Single Woman 50

Chapter 5: Excellent Finance Tips for Women 53

Conclusion 55

Check Out My Other Books 56

Finances Box Set #8: Debt Free Forever + Money Management Makeover + Single Women & Finances

Introduction

I want to thank you and congratulate you for purchasing the book, "Single Women & Finances: A Woman's Secret Diary To Saving, Budgeting, and Retirement"

This book contains proven steps and strategies on how to be financially secure in the future.

Because more and more women are opting to become single and enjoy their independence, this book empowers them to take better control of their finances so that they enjoy their lives even when they retire. It takes single women to a journey of saving, budgeting, and retirement planning. This book shares some great and practical tips so that single women enjoy their lives without draining their purses and bank accounts.

Thanks again for purchasing this book, I hope you enjoy it!

Chapter 1: Advantages and Disadvantages of Being a Single Woman

For the 21st Century, being single can equate to happiness and satisfaction. Currently, a lot of women opt to stay single. Marriage is no longer considered a necessity. The woman of today isn't afraid of not having a husband. Today, she can even have a home and a child without a man in her life. Although cultures differ, more and more women have embraced a solitary life.

A single woman is more physically fit because she has time to go to the gym. She has exercise groups to keep her attractive and slim. On the contrary, married women gain weight because they don't have time to work out. In fact, unhappy married women are observed to gain more weight. A single woman can achieve greater things because she has no responsibility to a family. She has more time to spend in her career. A single woman has less housework to do because she doesn't have to tend to an untidy spouse and children. Furthermore, a single woman can manage her own money. She's not saddled with debts of an irresponsible husband. She's well-rested. She gets more sleep, thus enhancing her cognitive and memory skills. A single woman doesn't have a lot of mental health issues because she only worries about herself. She has time to meet old and new friends. She's not burdened by the demands of marriage and motherhood.

A single woman takes better trips. She can do interesting activities while on vacation. She can also meet more interesting people in the process. She knows herself better. She knows what she wants in life. She doesn't have to explain to anyone why she came home late and who was with her. She has time for herself, her career, and her hobbies. People who are into a relationship have to include that certain person into their daily routine. Thus, they become less focused and less available for activities for self-improvement. A single woman finds her life less stressful. Although relationships bring fulfillment and joy, finding the right man can be difficult. A lot of people who are in relationships find it stressful as they try to keep a balance. They go to therapists to improve the quality of their lives. These people often forget about their dreams and wishes because they focus their energy and efforts in making their partners happy. A single woman doesn't have to deal with such stress. In fact, she can even engage in stress-relieving activities because she has the freedom and time to do so.

This type of woman doesn't have to deal with the constraints placed by her partner or family. She is not bound by the hypocrisy she has to put up with. She doesn't have to spend her day off having lunch or going shopping with her husband's sister or mother when she's rather have time for her girlfriends. She doesn't have to be dragged to the house of her partner's parents for a holiday dinner. She can stay at home with a good book instead of pretending to have a nice meal with people she doesn't like. A single woman's time is hers alone. She doesn't have to fit her schedule with that of her husband or family. She can go shopping or go out to dinner anytime she wants. She can go straight to bed if she wants to. She decides how to spend her money. She doesn't have to prioritize the needs of someone else over her own. She makes financial decisions by herself.

Because she's single, the woman can pursue a career. She can spend long hours to get ahead in her career without feeling guilty that she doesn't have time for her partner or family. She can go on a cruise or a road trip. She can gain a perspective of what she really wants in her life, in her partner, or in her family.

Disadvantages of Being a Single Woman

The feeling of being alone or lonely will usually pop up when the single woman is facing a big problem, going through holidays, or having an illness. If she has no one to celebrate a milestone with or she doesn't have someone to share her secrets, she feels alone. Furthermore, she'll be distressed if she has no dare to dinner parties or a wedding. She also lacks intimacy. As she gets older, she'll find it difficult to find a partner. In addition, a single woman has to do everything on her own. She has to do the household chores, run the errands, and all other things that must be done. Living alone can also be very expensive. If a woman is single, she gets no financial assistance to pay her bills and rent. If she doesn't have budgeting skills, she will experience financial constraints. It is a challenge for her to keep her finances in order. A single woman doesn't get additional benefits in housing, insurance, etc. She even has to pay a higher income tax. In addition, she can't avail of 2-for-1 offers. She has to pay the full price for a cruise or a hotel room. More importantly, she has to take extra precaution. She may be robbed or maimed if she's not careful.

Chapter 2: Saving Tips for a Single Woman

Currently, there are more single women than married ones. There are many single women who earn a lot of money. They now make better financial decisions. However, most of these women still feel inadequate to navigate their financial life successfully. They struggle because they have no formal training in money management. They grow up believing a lot of money myths which caused anxiety, feeling of inadequacy, and confusion. They can't remain in one job for a long time. They usually have careers that didn't offer a lot of earning potential like administrative work and teaching. They have no confidence about the math of money management. They also prefer investing in relationships rather than investing in financial security. Lastly, these single women are often victims of wage and financial discrimination.

It is important for a single woman to take control of her finances because she has to make ends meet. She has no partner to share the expenses with. She has to repay her debts. She has to have insurance and/or savings to continue paying the bills if she becomes disabled, injured, or sick. She is primarily responsible for her retirement savings. Lastly, her future or long term expenses will increase while her earning ability will decrease over time.

Tax Savings for a Single Woman

As a single taxpayer, a woman must plan her actions for the year in order to minimize her taxable income and maximize her tax deductions. She can look for tax savings at her job, her home, her school and other expenses, her family planning, her inheritance, and her retirement savings and investments.

At work, she can work out on her W-4 form if she got a huge tax refund for the year because it means that her employer is deducting a lot of tax from her paycheck regularly. By filing a new form, she can get more money at the time she earns it. It can mean an additional $225 monthly. If the employer offers a flex plan, a single woman must avail of it because she can use a portion of her salary to a medical reimbursement account which can be used to pay medical bills. With this strategy, she can't be charged Social Security and income tax for her account contribution. She saves as much as 35%. She can contribute a maximum of $2,500 to her flex plan.

If the single woman doesn't want to concern herself with higher taxes in the future, she can move her retirement contributions to a Roth 401(k) if it's offered by her employer. The Roth 401(k) doesn't offer a tax break. However, if she withdraws from her Roth 401(k), she doesn't get taxed. If she's unemployed, she can monitor her job-hunting costs so that she can deduct such costs from her taxable income provided that it isn't her first job and that she's seeking a new position in a similar line of work. The cost of overnight accommodation if she has to search outside of her state can be deducted as miscellaneous expenses if the costs don't go beyond 2% of the adjusted gross income.

Moving costs because of a new job can also be deducted from taxable income if the new job is outside the 50-mile radius from her old home. If she uses her own car in moving to her new home, she can subtract 23.5 cents per mile plus tolls and parking. She can also save tax money if she opts to pay tax on the value of her restricted stock as soon as she receives it. A restricted stock can be offered by an employer as a fringe benefit. If she pays immediately instead of waiting for the shares of stock to vest, she can pay a lower tax because the value of the stock may be lower at the time she receives it than at the time the shares are fully vested. The 401(k) loan must be repaid before the single woman resigns from her job. If she doesn't, the loan will be treated as a distribution and will be taxed at the top bracket. She will also pay a 10% penalty if she leaves the job before she turns 55 years old. There are employers who provide educational assistance to their employees at a maximum amount of $5,250 tax-free.

The single woman can buy her first home from her Roth IRA. She won't be penalized or taxed if she withdraws from her account, provided the distribution doesn't exceed $10,000 worth of earnings and the account has been existing for 5 years already. However, the whole Roth IRA contributions can be used as down payment for the house. Educational expenses for training and graduate studies can qualify as Lifetime Learning Credit, which is equivalent to 20% of the expenses or a maximum of $10,000. However, the single woman can't claim the benefit if she earns more than $50,000 a year. Furthermore, she can deduct expenses even if she doesn't itemize them. The standard deduction can be used if it's larger than the total itemized expenses. If her parents didn't claim the interest deductions for her student loan, the single woman can use them even if she doesn't itemize.

If the single woman is a beneficiary of a 401(k) plan, she can roll it over to an IRA account with pay outs stretched over her lifetime. Furthermore, if she has investments, it is best for her to consult the calendar prior to selling her holdings. If she wants to be eligible to a preferential tax rate, she must sell her investments ate least a year after she bought them. Before buying shares of a mutual fund towards the end of the year, she must know when the fund will pay out dividends. If she buys shares before the payout, she'll receive the dividend but she has to pay tax for it, on the other hand, if she waits after the payout, she'll be able to buy shares at a lower price and she won't have to pay any tax. Lastly, the IRA contributions must be made as soon as possible so that she can file tax-deferred returns. If she has a Roth IRA, the returns are tax-exempt.

Chapter 3: Budget Tips for the Single Woman

Creating a Budget

Everyone must know how to budget their money. For a single woman, budgeting becomes a requisite because no one will monitor her finances but herself. As such, it is important to create a budget for a better future.

The first step in creating a budget is to analyze her present financial status. She can do this by checking all her bank accounts as well as all her debts. In assessing his finances, she must include the car loan, student loan, and credit cards. Furthermore, she must know how much she has in retirement accounts, stocks, and other investments. Next, she has to account for her total bills in a month. She can check her bank statement if she doesn't keep her bills. From those bills, she can determine her monthly consumption of utilities and other regular expenditures. Loan amortization is also included in the list. In addition, she must list her monthly expenses on groceries, shopping, entertainment, and other irregular expenses. From the list of regular and irregular expenses, she'll have an idea how much she spends monthly. She can set a limit for these expenses to control her spending.

The third step is to start saving. A savings account is an indispensable way to start budgeting. It should be reserved for emergencies or important and large purchases. According to financial advisors, the savings account must have about 3-6 months' worth of salary. Next, the debts must be paid monthly. The single woman must ensure to make larger payments to her loans and credit cards so that interest payments will be reduced. Finally, she must monitor her bank accounts and adjust her budget if she finds that she's making more withdrawals.

Steps to Create a Budget

It is important for every single woman to determine her monthly expenses. What she can do is list down all her expenses in a month. It is important that she keeps the receipts. She can have the list on a worksheet file or in a notebook. She should categorize her spending into groceries, entertainment, electric bill, gas and transportation, dining out, rent, and utilities. The categories must be listed in a horizontal manner while the amounts must be listed adjacent to the categories. The amounts are then totaled at the end.

After making the column total, it is important to evaluate the expenses. Some categories can be necessary expenses but expenses in non-essential categories must be trimmed down. Each spending category must have a goal so that she can start saving for her emergency fund. At least 10% of her income must be saved for emergencies. After creating the budget, it must be tracked to ensure that she's spending within her budget. There are online applications which can help her track her spending. Lastly, the budget must be re-evaluated if she's not reaching her financial goals.

Budgeting Tools Every Single Woman Can Use

The single woman can still make use of the envelope system. She can use virtual or real envelopes to keep her money for variable expenses like dining out and entertainment. If she has already spent her money in the envelope, she has to wait for the next payday to refill the envelope. There are certain expenses which can use automatic drafts. The 401(k) contributions are automatically deducted by the employer while the IRA contributions can be withdrawn automatically from a checking account. The single woman will only have to make arrangements with her bank about automatic drafts. This method is effective because she won't be tempted to spend the money if it is automatically deducted from her account. Lastly, she can take advantage of money market accounts to park emergency fund. This account has high yield and can be accessed easily in emergencies.

Chapter 4: Retirement Tips for the Single Woman

A single woman needs to make important retirement plans. Because she's single, her financial security during her retirement must be of greater significance. She has to know how to make use of all available resources for this purpose. Not a lot of people plan their retirement. They don't have enough savings to use during their retirement. They don't even maximize their Social Security benefits. In reality, people plan their vacations but not their future.

To save for retirement, a realistic analysis of financial resources must be done so that the single woman can make her most important decisions. She needs to find out ways to cut her expenses in order to save money for her retirement. Some people hire a financial advisor to help them. If she's taking advantage of this service, she has to ensure that she pays the advisor a fixed fee rather than a transaction charge or commission. Furthermore, the advisor must have the necessary credentials to prove his expertise in retirement planning.

Upon her retirement, the single woman will rely mostly on her Social Security benefits. Therefore, it is a must that she maximizes its use. It is important to claim the benefit until she has exhausted all her other sources of retirement income because money from Social Security increases substantially for each year the claim is delayed. The 401(k) and IRA accounts can be used to generate income. A lot of individuals spend their retirement as they please so that the sources of income become depleted even before they die. It is advisable for the single woman to study the different ways to generate retirement income so that she can choose the best alternative for her needs.

Another important tip is for her to ensure that she takes care of her health. Diseases and ailments can be costly and disabling. As such, the single woman must exercise and eat a balanced diet. Although there is no guarantee that she won't get sick during her retirement, she'll recover faster is she's in a better health condition. Lastly, she can surround herself with caring family and friends. She can't be threatened by extreme loneliness if she's in the company of friends and relatives. She can live with friends or relatives to share the costs of living.

Decisions Every Single Woman Must Make

A single woman must make career decisions. Because retirees can have about 30 more years in their lives, a single female must ensure that she still has money to spend for a long retirement period. Therefore, she can plan her career so that she can still continue to work even when she's in her 70s. At her 40s, she can develop the intellectual skills, earning potential, and expertise so that she can still be productive even at an old age. She also has to make investing decisions. If she's putting money in retirement plans, she can decide to put the money in investments to earn more money. When she retires, she needs to replace lost income. She can assess investments based on risk-return trade offs. When she is nearing retirement, she has to make investing decisions. She can't take risk with her investments because she can't afford to lose money.

In addition, the single woman has to decide how she will claim her Social Security benefits. In general, a woman can claim against her husband's Social Security benefits. She can even claim against the Social Security benefits of her ex-husband if they've been married for at least 10 years. More often than not, women are also their husband's beneficiary so they can claim spousal benefits. On the other hand, a single woman doesn't have spousal benefits so the best alternative is to delay claiming her Social Security benefits so that her money can still generate more returns. Lastly, a single woman must decide on long-term care. She must consider being strong and healthy even when she's already retired. She has to take advantage of long-term care insurance so that she can avail of in-home care services later in her life. She can also plan on gathering social resources to keep her company during retirement.

Deciding Where to Retire

Retirement has changed in various ways. Today, couples in their 50s may end up as single individuals upon retirement. Some may be divorced. Others remain unmarried while the rest may have lost their spouse because of unfortunate death. A single woman can choose to retire overseas if she wants to mingle and mix with expats. She can choose a country with interesting people, fun activities, and low cost of living. She must search for places where there are expat communities, events, and activities which help her to stay active. Furthermore, the location must be safe for single women like her. She can start looking for such communities through online forums. She can meet a lot of people online even before she moves or visits the country. She can also search for volunteer groups to help her connect with the expat community and the local people. If she's into hobbies, she can start looking for hobby groups.

A single woman can still date during retirement although she may have a different purpose than a 20-year-old or a 30-year-old woman. She doesn't look for a man whom she can start a family with. She just looks for a man she can have fun with. At retirement age, a lot people already had a lot of experiences with ex-spouses and children. Most of them had failed marriages while others became caregivers of their sick partner. Therefore, most retirees don't want to enter a new relation because they feel they will be obligated again. They experienced physical and emotional losses. Therefore, most of them put up a wall when intimacy is concerned. Successful dating can open up willingness and commitment to move forward even if they feel anxious and vulnerable. A single woman may find it difficult to date during retirement because there are more single women than single men.

In the United States of America, single retirees are often in metro areas of New Orleans and Miami. Most retirees in these locations are single. Divorce rates are also high in the two locations. The metro areas of New York; Memphis, Tennessee; and Jackson, Mississippi also have a large number of single seniors.

Finances Box Set #8: Debt Free Forever + Money Management Makeover + Single Women & Finances

In Ogden, Utah, the place had the lowest number of single seniors at 29.3% while metro areas like Boise, Idaho; Lancaster, Pasadena; and Cape Coral, Florida have about 33% of the total retirees' population comprising of single retirees. There are more single women retirees than men because they outlive their husbands. A single woman can move out of her current social network to start the process of meeting new friends. She can go into online dating, attend a new church, or try new hobbies to meet new friends.

Chapter 5: Excellent Finance Tips for Women

Most people live differently now compared to people from past generations. Individuals wait a long time before they marry and start a family. Thus, it is not surprising to find a lot of single women nowadays. Furthermore, because the divorce rate is increasing, a lot of women become single once again. Gender roles can be a factor why there a lot of women who put their needs aside to fulfill the needs of their husbands and their children. As such, they don't consider their own personal finances to secure their retirement.

A single woman must create a budget and try her very best to stick to it. Actually, budgeting applies to everyone. She must assess her monthly expenses without forgetting esthetics, utilities, gas, car amortization, insurance, groceries, utilities, and housing costs. The same must be done with her income. The expenses are then subtracted from her income to know how much is left. The remainder is then divided into her discretionary spending and savings. Payments for debts like student loans and credit card debts must also be included in the list of expenses. Debts must be cleared as soon as possible so that she doesn't have to pay interests on these loans. She has to reduce her expenses in order to have more money to pay her debts.

A lot of women are known to be impulse shoppers. It can be difficult for them not to buy things on impulse but impulse buying must be avoided. Emotional spending must be avoided as well. Unnecessary expenses must be limited in order for a single woman to improve her personal finances. She must make it a point not to use her credit card to buy these non-essentials. As such as possible, she has to stay true to her budget. To do so, she has to wait at least a day to decide whether to buy a non-essential item or not. If she doesn't want to buy it the next day, she made a great effort to stay away from impulse buying.

Unfortunate events can occur in everyone's life. A single woman can't expect her life to be a bed of roses at all times. As such, she has to have money for emergencies. Home or car repairs, or unexpected illness, can be a huge burden. If it's an illness, she may not be able to work for a long time. She need not worry about money if she has saved some for the rainy days. She can start by saving a few bucks a day. Before she knows it, she has accumulated a lot of money already. She can keep her emergency fund in a high-interest savings account. If she has saved for the fund already, her excess money can be used for investing so that she'll earn more money. As a word of caution, the single woman mustn't keep her hopes up. Her expectations must be realistic. The single woman must set a realistic amount for her savings account so that she doesn't sacrifice her other needs.

Every individual wants to own a home. For most people, a home is an investment which can be rewarding in the future. If the single woman is currently renting an apartment, she may think of using the rental money to pay for her own home instead of paying it to her landlord. However, she must first consider if she can afford to buy a house. She also has to think of her own safety. The new home and community must be a safe place for single women like her. She also needs to consider if she'll accept roommates so that they can help pay for the monthly amortization. Next, she has to think what she'll do with the house if she marries and starts a family. To help her decide, she can make a list of what she can afford and what she wants in a house before contacting an agent. She can opt for a town house or a condominium because it is smaller and easy to maintain. Furthermore, it is cheaper than a stand-alone house. She must remember that a condominium or a town house is just a temporary home for her. She can buy a large house as she becomes more financially stable. Furthermore, her needs may change in the future. Thus, she can think of her first home as a way of building equity and establishing herself.

Because everyone eventually grows old, the single woman must think of her retirement even at an early stage. It isn't just short-term goals which define financial security. It is also important to think about long-term goals even if she wants to remain single until she retires. She has to take care of herself. Her budget must allow her to save money for her retirement. Her retirement savings plan can either be paid up using lump sum or monthly contributions.

A single woman mustn't be afraid to invest her money. When she has accumulated cash in her savings account, she can use the extra money to invest in viable investments so that she'll earn more money. She mustn't be scared even if she is not an expert in finance. She has to believe in herself. She can hire the services of a financial advisor or an investment manager to help her with her investing needs. From her initial capital, she can earn more money which she can use to maintain her lifestyle even if she's retired. There are risks but there are also big rewards. She must have the courage to act. She can spend some time researching about investments and pick out investment vehicles according to her risk appetite.

She must not forget to enjoy her life. She's allowed to spoil herself from time to time. She can go on a vacation, spend a day at the spa, or buy something special for herself. These things can be investments on her own happiness and in herself. She needs to reward herself after all her hard work in maintaining balance in her life. Furthermore, she must ensure that such special treats are within her budget. She doesn't have to be deep in debt because of these rewards.

Lastly, if ever the single woman decides to get married in the future, she has to sit down with her partner to talk about money before they take the plunge. They may feel excited about their wedding and forget to agree on essential matters first. The single woman must know how much her future husband earns, his debts, and his future financial plans. By taking the wedding vows, both parties agree to be financial partners. As such, she needs to know if their spending habits and financial habits jibe with each other. She has to ensure that he won't financially drain her and destroy whatever financial success she's enjoying before she gets married.

Conclusion

Thank you again for purchasing this book!

I hope this book was able to help you to become a better person by empowering you to take charge of your financed.

The next step is to try the practical tips listed in this book.

Finally, if you enjoyed this book, please take the time to share your thoughts and post a review on Amazon. We do our best to reach out to readers and provide the best value we can. Your positive review will help us achieve that. It'd be greatly appreciated!

Thank you and good luck!

Check Out My Other Books

Below you'll find some of my other popular books that are popular on Amazon and Kindle as well. Simply click on the links below to check them out. Alternatively, you can visit my author page on Amazon to see other work done by me.

Marketing Money Mastery

http://amzn.to/1hxUaj6

"Debt Free Forever"

http://amzn.to/1qrgldh

Money Management Makeover

http://amzn.to/1hAU8Z7

Single Women and Budgets

http://amzn.to/WPRJ3M

www.ingramcontent.com/pod-product-compliance
Lightning Source LLC
Chambersburg PA
CBHW071818170526
45167CB00003B/1359